LEARN TO DRAW

Disney
PRINCESS

THE LITTLE
MERMAID

Illustrated by The Disney Storybook Artists

Walter Foster

1 3 5 7 9 10 8 6 4 2

Table of Contents

The Story of The Little Mermaid

Ariel is a fun-loving and mischievous mermaid enchanted with all things human. She loves to explore underwater shipwrecks and find ancient "treasures" with her best friend, a chatty, loveable fish named Flounder. Her father King Triton, ruler of the merpeople, charges Sebastian, a reggae-singing Caribbean crab, with chaperoning Ariel and making sure she stays out of trouble.

One day, Ariel disobeys her father's orders to stay away from the world above the sea and swims to the surface. In a sudden raging storm, she rescues the prince of her dreams. Completely love-struck by this handsome stranger, Ariel's wish to become a human grows even stronger. Determined to reach this goal, she strikes a bargain with the devious sea witch Ursula and trades her fins and beautiful voice for legs.

Ursula tells Ariel that she has just three days to win Prince Eric's heart, or their deal will become permanent. Scared and unsure how her new legs work, yet thrilled to finally be on land, Ariel embarks on a courageous mission to try and make Prince Eric remember her and fall deeply in love—all without being able to say a single word! With the help of Flounder and Sebastian, Ariel is able to regain her voice, capture her prince's heart, and save her father's kingdom from Ursula's evil threats—all in one heart-pounding race against time!

Tools & Materials

You'll need only a few supplies to create all of your favorite characters from *The Little Mermaid*. You may prefer working with a drawing pencil to begin with, and it's always a good idea to have a pencil sharpener and an eraser nearby. When you've finished drawing, you can add color with felt-tip markers, colored pencils, watercolors, or acrylic paint. The choice is yours!

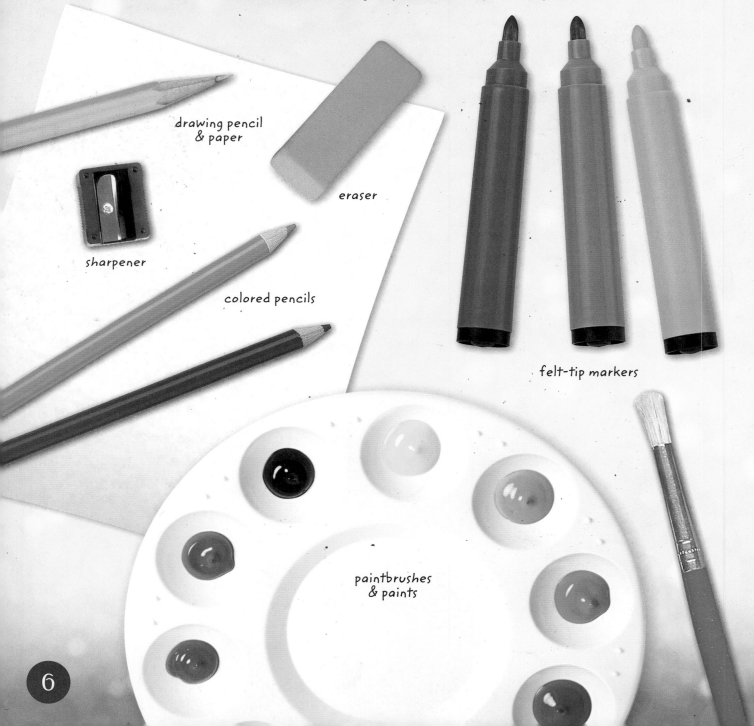

drawing pencil & paper

eraser

sharpener

colored pencils

felt-tip markers

paintbrushes & paints

How to Use this Book

In this book you'll learn to draw your favorite characters in just a few simple steps. You'll also get lots of helpful tips from Disney artists that will guide you through the drawing process. With a little practice, you'll soon be producing successful drawings of your own!

First draw the basic shapes, using light lines that will be easy to erase.

Each new step is shown in blue, so you'll know what to draw next.

Follow the blue lines to draw the details.

Now darken the lines you want to keep, and erase the rest.

Use some magic (or crayons or markers) to add color to your drawing!

Ariel

The three-quarter view is the best angle to use to make
a character look three-dimensional. Notice how much depth, form,
and structure can be achieved in this drawing of Ariel's head.

People around the world have been charmed by Ariel's cheerful enthusiasm. Be sure to show some of her energy when drawing her complete figure. A strong line of action will help give the feeling that Ariel's body flows naturally into her graceful tail!

NO!

YES!

give her tail natural-
looking movement

4

5

Ariel is
6 heads tall

Ariel's personality, mannerisms, and charm all come to life with the right action poses. Make sure her adventurous, cheerful spirit is clear in your drawing.

Ariel's profile is curvy

NO!

YES!

1

2

3

YES! NO!

Ariel has an upturned nose

Ariel is so excited to become a human and try out her new legs.
She hopes Prince Eric will notice her without her voice, so make sure
her very first gown is fit for a beautiful princess!

Prince Eric

Eric's handsome looks capture Ariel's heart so much that she is willing to change her whole life to be with him. Make sure you draw him standing proudly, like the strong prince he is.

8

Eric is a brave, athletic prince who loves the high seas. Make sure to show his love for adventure when drawing him in an action pose.

NO! YES!

Sebastian

Sebastian is a little crab with a big voice and a big heart. Try to bring out the warmer side of his personality when you draw him.

Sebastian is
6 heads tall

4

5

When drawing Sebastian in action, notice that his hard shell does not change shape—instead, it is his flexible face and legs that twist and stretch when he is feeling festive!

YES!

NO!

4

5

Flounder

Flounder's spunk and vulnerability are the qualities
that make him so memorable. Use this three-quarter view to
show all the depth of his chubby cheeks and oval nose.

4

Out →
In →

In →
Out →

5

Out
In
Out
In

Because Flounder doesn't have any limbs to draw, his face has to show a lot of emotion. He is always up for an exciting adventure with Ariel, and he is loyal enough to swim to her rescue in any kind of danger.

YES! NO!

Scuttle

Scuttle the seagull is a loveable, goofy character. His eyes are usually crossed underneath his thick, dark eyebrows, and he is overweight and scruffy. Draw Scuttle with full, feathery cheeks.

King Triton

King Triton is a loving father who would do anything to protect his daughters and the people in his underwater kingdom. He is a strict ruler, but he has a generous, kind heart.

King Triton is
9 heads tall

YES!

NO!

7

8

9

Ursula

Ursula manipulates everyone to get what she wants. She is selfish (not shellfish), but even though she steals Ariel's voice, she never steals the song in Ariel's heart.

Ursula has six tentacles (or "legs") instead of eight

Detail of her shell earrings

Detail on shell around her neck

53

5

6

Ursula has three
eyelashes on the
top lid and two on
the bottom

her brows have a high arch;
they are thicker in the center
and taper to a point

Flotsam & Jetsam

These two eels are Ursula's minions who spy, steal, and trick others on her behalf.
Be sure to show their cruel and cunning character when drawing them.

Jetsam has a dead
left eye

Flotsam has a dead
right eye

Chef Louis

Chef Louis is head chef in Prince Eric's palace. When Ariel arrives, he prepares a delicious feast; the only problem is, he'd like to boil Sebastian to be part of it!

Grimsby

Grimsby is a loyal and helpful advisor to Prince Eric. Try to incorporate his formal, proper stance into your drawing.

Grimsby is
6 heads tall

Max

Max is always by Prince Eric's side, and he is full of enthusiasm!
He likes Ariel from the moment he meets her and gives her
a slobbery welcome.

5

YES!   NO!

6

The End

Now that you've learned the secrets to drawing your favorite characters from *The Little Mermaid*, try creating different scenes from the underwater and human worlds in the film. With your pencil, paper, and a little imagination, even the wildest of dreams can come true!